A Listen to
JAZZ

Written by
Colleen Hord

Rourke
Educational Media

rourkeeducationalmedia.com

www.rourkeeducationalmedia.com

PHOTO CREDITS: Cover: © Emilie Duchesne (front), © Mlenny Photography (back); page 1: © portishead1; page 3: © slobo; pages 4, 5, 12, 14, 15, 17, 19: Library of Congress; page 6: © bikeriderlondon; page 7: © StephanHoerold; page 8: © Vira Mylyan-Monastyrska; page 9: © Anna Bryukhanova (top left), © Ysbrand Cosijn (top right), © sandsun (bottom left), © DeshaCAM (bottom right); page 10: © Ysbrand Cosijn; page 11: © Paolo Cipriani; page 13: © Bob Sacha; page 16: © Martin Yu; pages 18, 19: © PhotoHouse; page 20: © cristianl; page 21: © lev radin; page 22: © AndreyPopov

Edited by Precious McKenzie

Cover and Interior design by Tara Raymo

Library of Congress PCN Data

A Listen to Jazz / Colleen Hord
 (Art and Music)
  ISBN 978-1-62169-880-7 (hard cover)
  ISBN 978-1-62169-775-6 (soft cover)
  ISBN 978-1-62169-980-4 (e-Book)
Library of Congress Control Number: 2013936789

Also Available as:
ROURKE'S
e-Books

Rourke Educational Media
Printed in the United States of America,
North Mankato, Minnesota

Rourke
Educational Media

rourkeeducationalmedia.com

customerservice@rourkeeducationalmedia.com • PO Box 643328 Vero Beach, Florida 32964

Table of Contents

America's Music

Ragtime, swing, **scat**, be bop, and Dixie. What do all of those silly sounding words have in common? They are all related to a type of music called jazz. Jazz was born in the late 1700s when Africans, who were brought to America as slaves, used field songs to communicate with one another.

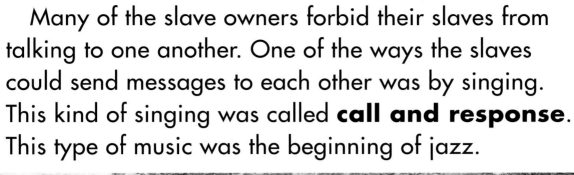

Many of the slave owners forbid their slaves from talking to one another. One of the ways the slaves could send messages to each other was by singing. This kind of singing was called **call and response**. This type of music was the beginning of jazz.

When working, one slave would sing out a statement and another would sing back the answer.

Call and response songs were usually about freedom or news about family. This way of communicating turned into a more spiritual type of song, which was the beginning of gospel music. Gospel music is also a form of jazz.

Just as America is made up of many different people from around the world, so is jazz. Jazz echoes the influences of many cultures.

The Sounds of Jazz

Jazz has a very unique sound because it can take on many forms. Jazz is also known for the way musicians **improvise**.

When singing or playing jazz, musicians follow the melody. When they feel a different musical mood come over them, or if they think adding some notes would make a different statement, they improvise the sound.

Saxophone

Trumpet

Electric guitar

Piano

When musicians play the saxophone or other jazz instruments they answer the other players in the band with improvised notes.

Jazz soloists make up nonsense words or sounds called scat and substitute new words in place of the written words. Sometimes the singers even make musical instrument sounds with their voices.

Another component of jazz is **syncopation**.
Syncopation is a rhythmic accent on an unexpected beat.

The accent in music is usually placed on the first and third beats, which are the strongest. With syncopation, the accent is placed on the weaker second and fourth beats.

Congo Square

The city of New Orleans, Louisiana played an important role in the history of jazz. Slaves and freed slaves were allowed to meet on Sundays. They gathered together to visit, sell market items, dance, drum, and sing. The place they met was called Congo Square.

You can still visit Congo Square in New Orleans' Louis Armstrong Park. Congo Square is now a historical landmark. Every year people gather there to attend jazz festivals.

LOUIS ARMSTRONG 1901-1971

The Louis Armstrong Park was named after the famous jazz singer and trumpeter from New Orleans. Louis Armstrong was also known for the way he imitated a musical instrument with his voice. This jazz technique was called scat. Armstrong was the first to record it. Louis Armstrong died in 1971. His music, including the song *What a Wonderful World*, is still very popular today.

Musicians in Congo Square keep African music alive in New Orleans.

13

Jazz in America's History

In 1863, slavery was abolished. Former slaves migrated north to cities like Chicago and New York. Soon jazz started spreading across the United States.

SCOTT JOPLIN 1867·1917

Scott Joplin is known as the King of Ragtime. He was born in 1867 and was first introduced to the piano at a home where his mother was a housekeeper. Joplin started his musical career in the 1880s but wasn't recognized for all his contributions to jazz and the world of music until fifty years after his death. The most famous ragtime piano piece of all time is Joplin's *Maple Leaf Rag*.

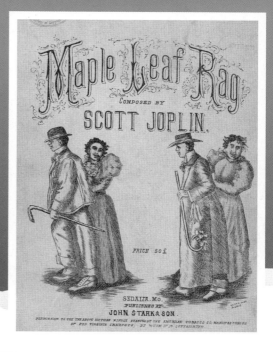

Irving Berlin (1888-1989) was one of the United States' most popular songwriters. His first big hit was the ragtime song Alexander's Ragtime Band.

The mixture of European and Caribbean influences, along with African-American music, created a new sound of jazz. This new sound was called ragtime. Ragtime was known for its syncopation.

In the 1920s there were many jazz nightclubs where jazz artists performed. Once **phonographs** and radios became popular, more people became familiar with jazz.

In the 1930s and 1940s, America went through some hard times. First, there was the Great **Depression**. Many people were out of work. Many Americans were homeless. Not too long after the Great Depression, America went to war.

The money many people had saved or invested was lost due to banks closing and the stock market crashing.

One thing that helped cheer people up was jazz music. Just like when the slaves sang their field songs to cheer each other up, jazz music on the radio helped people take their minds off their problems.

ELLA FITZGERALD
1917 - 1996

Ella Fitzgerald was born in 1917. She was an orphan in her teen years. After winning a talent contest she was on her way to becoming one of the greatest singers in jazz history. Even people who weren't familiar with jazz loved to listen to her rich voice. She was nicknamed "Scat Mama" for the way she used scat in her singing. She died in 1996.

Jazz Today

Today jazz continues to thrive. Many schools have jazz choirs and jazz bands. Cities all over America have jazz festivals.

Maybe you can join a jazz music program at your school. The world of jazz has a bright future and you could be part of it whether you are listening to or performing the soulful sounds of jazz.

Musicians carry on the jazz tradition. The very nature of jazz allows it to grow into something new, yet very familiar.

With all the cultural, regional, and musical changes, jazz has become an influential part of the music we listen to today.

Glossary

call and reponse (kawl-and-RI-spons): musical communication where one voice or instrument makes a statement and another answers it

depression (di-PRESH-uhn): a time when businesses do badly and many people become poor

improvise (IM-pruh-vise): making up words or music on the spot

phonographs (FOH-nu-grafs): machines that reproduce sounds that have been recorded on records

ragtime (RAG-time): an early style of jazz having a strong, syncopated rhythm

scat (SCAT): vocal improvisation using nonsense words or syllables to imitate instruments

syncopation (SING-kuh-pay-shuhn): a rhythmic accent on an unexpected beat

Index

Websites

www.pbskids.org/jazz

www.smithsonianjazz.org

www.neajazzintheschools.org

About the Author

Colleen Hord is an elementary teacher. Her favorite part of her teaching day is Writer's Workshop. She enjoys kayaking, walking on the beach, and collecting just the right river rocks to write words of inspiration on for her word garden.

Meet The Author!
www.meetREMauthors.com